Human Behavior Power!
By John Mind

Understanding the Power of Self Esteem, Mind Control, Manipulation, and Deception to Get What You Want!
2nd Edition

Table of Contents

Introduction

I want to thank you and congratulate you for purchasing the book, *"Human Behavior Power! Understanding the Power of Self Esteem, Mind Control, Manipulation, and Deception to Get What You Want!"*

This book contains proven steps and strategies on how to steer other people into the direction you want them to be heading. Influencing and controlling others can be beneficial or disruptive depending on the employment method used and most importantly the intent that is behind the need or desire to influence others.

This book aims to shed light to the concepts of manipulation, mind control and deception. A strong foundation for an effective implementation of human behavior control or manipulation is sufficient knowledge; hence, this book provides discussions of the nature and wonders of the said motivating actions.

In addition, this book contains information on people's "blind spots" so you would know how to position yourself better when it comes to getting them to see your point, or just to defend your stance. The power of suggestion would be discussed in detail as well.

Thanks again for purchasing this book. I hope you enjoy it!

Chapter 1 – Influencing the Human Behavior

Man is probably the only living being in this planet that takes pride in the fact that he capable of rational and independent thinking. However, the concept of freewill has been a hot subject for psychologists and philosophers. Is it even possible for men to have free thought and ability to make independent decisions when they are capable of being influenced?

The Problem of Freewill

One of the classic problems of philosophy is the idea of independent reason – is mankind really capable of deciding for his own good, or is man just a product of circumstances that greatly control the decisions that he would be making?

If you are going to go back to the history of psychology and neuroscience, there is great evidence that freewill probably does not exist at all – independent decisions are actually made of pre-conditioning and action-reaction triggers that the brain has to ensure the body's sustainability. The moment that you have decided to turn on the coffee pot every start of the day is all because of habits that lead to that action.

However, it is not easy to accept that man is not an independently rational being. To believe that man is not capable of using his mind independently makes it seem that man is not responsible for anything that has happened throughout the course of history. Without the notion of independence, society's notion of justice and fairness would seize to exist. When you think about it, it makes a person's life rather bleak and very animalistic. However, you would argue that there are too many things that make you different from any other living thing out there that just exists towards the end of their lifespan. You dream and believe in certain truths about life, and for that reason, you are able to understand metaphysical concepts such as happiness, equality and self-actualization. You can equate these concepts to be more valuable than putting food in your mouth. It is also very important to keep in mind that these concepts are only made possible for any being that has the ability to think about goodness and the importance of the self.

So how do you solve the problem of free will's existence? To most philosophers and psychologists, the answer is simple – man's mind is able to adapt, and a person is not largely made up of a series of experiences. That is why mankind is special – they are able to build beliefs based on what they experience and they are able to see what is right from wrong. When man sticks to the idea that he is free and he is moral, he becomes a person not just motivated with survival but also with his definition of his self.

Man versus Influence

If human rationality does exist, it is still possible for one's course of reason to change from time to time. This is made possible by the mind's ability to be influenced and be bent according to a particular purpose. A person's knowledge, or the things that he justified as true belief, can change according to what he experiences and how he interprets them. For this reason, it is possible for his environment and his society to dictate what he perceives to be true.

Human behavior manipulation is not an invention of the field of science called psychology. What most people fail to see is that manipulation and deception has its existence for as long as people started trying to influence each other. You can think of it as one of the faculties available to human beings to ensure survival, or simply because man is the only moving creature who embraces the culture of greed and power.

However, there are many situations when men benefit from influence, and here comes the human concept of obedience and social order. Strong social forces like the church and the government determined the significance of the power of influence. Hence, they have devoted much effort to understand, cultivate and generally benefit to what research reveals about social influence. In return, societies are able to build economies, quell civilian unrests, and also build governments that make peace possible. For long-established social authorities such as governments and religious orders, power and influence makes it possible for people to be united towards committing to a singular goal, which is why societies and cultures thrive.

The Idea of Belief

Several philosophers have also made it a point that the condition of human life can be harsh, and in order to successfully make peace and order possible, manipulation and deceit should be taken as necessary steps. Thomas Hobbes has questioned the possibility of social order due to the brutish nature of man. Niccolo Machiavelli's The Prince even described a good ruler to be a person who is not afraid of using covert tactics of instilling fear and uncertainty in people.

Some people claim that human behavior can easily be understood in terms of the stimulus-response model. However, some argue that such is way too simple to understand the complexity of the human mind and the human behavior. Nevertheless, science is powerful enough to have an objective understanding on how to manipulate even such a seemingly complicated process.

Ethical Limitations

While philosophers and social scientists has long pondered and upheld the idea of power and influence, there are several ethical concerns surround studies about social control and manipulation. It is simply not possible to have absolute order and equality among people when men make it a point to constantly manipulate and deceive each other for personal gain. While it is very possible for people to influence one another, it is very important for societies that this influence only extends to humane treatment of another person. Immanuel Kant made it a treatise that no person should treat another person as a means to an end, or that would be the end of any possible unity that governments and religions have established for centuries.

Hence, various research and experiments regarding mind control, manipulation and deception are rarely set out in the open. They are hidden elsewhere, away from the knowledge of the public. However, with the increasing access of people to information, thanks to technology, everyone can now read about the most covert tactics of manipulation and deceit.

However, knowing what manipulation and deceit really are makes it possible for people to also adjust to situations that make them extremely prone to these tactics. While it is still being argued whether people do have freewill and can actually make independent decisions, knowing when they are being steered away from making their own minds make it possible for them when they are being robbed of their right to be free.

For what is known, the invisible hand of social influence that steers people in a certain direction can be used even in small-scale scenarios. One does not need to control an entire crowd to maximize the capability of influencing the human behavior. Even in everyday living, manipulation, deception, mind control and other forms of motivating actions take place. It is almost everywhere now and most of the time, people under such strong kinds of influences are unaware that they are being controlled or manipulated. For these reason, the most dangerous practices of influence are undetectable. They are often practices that influence a person's subconscious, and then creates a path for a target to make decisions that lead to an influencer's benefit.

Understanding the power of influence and suggestion is crucial for a person to be able to utilize the phenomenon of human behavior manipulation. It is however important for a person to carry certain characteristics that could better his or her chances at influencing others. Manipulation can indeed be evil or good depending on how one uses it and the intent that lies beneath it. Hence, a person must have a very strong foundation called healthy sense of self and self-worth to be able to carry out his or her objectives without falling on his or her own pit.

Chapter 2 - Understanding Self-Esteem as a Psychological Resource

Various definitions can be used to describe what self-esteem is. It is not a new concept that carries significant ambiguity. Instead, it is a well-researched topic and this indicates how significant it is for human beings. One does not need to understand what self-esteem is to feel what it is like not to have an adequate amount of it. A person who feels incomplete, undeserving and lacking something is definitely suffering from an assaulted self-esteem.

A sense of self-worth is perhaps the simplest description that can be appropriated to the word self-esteem. It is the feeling and experience of being enough to be worthy of love, happiness and life. It is the confidence of a person that he or she is capable of thinking and coping with the life obstacles. A person with sufficient level of self-esteem knows that he or she is deserving and is entitled to want and need something.

Self-esteem is both a need and a resource for a person. A healthy self-esteem brings the feeling of security to a person. Someone with realistic confidence regarding his or her mind, capabilities and values can better deal with the world. Achieving success and happiness is not far from reality for an individual who has a healthy self-worth.

Why Is Self-Esteem Important?

Before, the significance of a healthy self-esteem is mainly correlated with the psychological wellbeing of the person. At present, however, a person's way of valuing his or her own worth is seen pivotal even for modern business. Indeed, a healthy self-esteem has now become an economic need.

A person with a low self-esteem is likely to limit his goals and ambitions. With the lacking self-efficacy and self-respect, a person cannot be as productive at work as he won't be effective in establishing smooth relationships with co-workers.

A healthy self-esteem is important for a person to reach his or her goals in life. Success can be influenced by the confidence a person has in the decisions he or she makes and actions he or she takes.

Although self-esteem sounds like a very personal matter, a person can clearly manifest it even on the outside. Indeed, several manifestations can be observed from a person who lacks confidence and self-respect.

The lack of self-esteem can easily be seen by the way a person carries him or herself in general. How a person walks, talks or even smile can reflect how little or how much confidence he or she has for him or herself.

A person with a healthy self-esteem is comfortable in discussing matters of accomplishments and even failures or shortcomings. He or she has no problem accepting and giving constructive criticisms or compliments. He or she is flexible enough to deal with different situations including challenging and stressful ones (Branden, 1992).

Accomplishments can be tied to a healthy self-esteem. It is more likely for a person with adequate confidence and self-belief to succeed in whatever he or she performs. Whether it is for personal growth, intimate relationship, professional development or even for manipulating and controlling other people, the significance of self-esteem is truly unquestionable.

Self-Esteem and Influential Abilities

There is no way that a person with low self-esteem will become able to pull off any magic trick or any other act of deception or manipulation. The reason is that self-esteem is that trait in humans that allow them to believe that they can influence another person.

At the same time, people who are targeted to be influenced can also be swayed to a particular direction if they can manage to trust the person whose goal is to influence them. Without this trust, a target would be very unlikely to believe anything that the other person is saying, or become compelled to do anything for the other person.

Self-esteem also enables a person to question whether a particular authority is right or not, and along with the knowledge he already has, makes him aware that he is being deceived or manipulated. For this reason, you may think that your belief in yourself and the things that you already know make you capable of combatting or enforcing control on another person. It is also the power that allows you to uphold your morals and make balance of your emotions and your intellect.

Chapter 3 – Self-Confidence and Power

In the earlier chapter, you have learned what self-esteem is and how important it is to build it in order to feel important and to be able to communicate well with other people. Now, it is time to learn how one's self-confidence is a source of power – in fact, it is the secret sauce of influence and manipulation.

Self-confidence, in itself, is not bad. However, when you review its meaning, its very definition has a strong connection to the idea of actually being important. To some people who have a strong sense of self-respect, they feel that they are even above other people, which grants them the entitlement that it is alright to influence and manipulate other people in order for them to subscribe to a set of belief or in order for them to be swayed into doing something that they would probably not do without someone influencing them. The morality of such act are many times put into question, and philosophers and psychologists say, time and again, that this is the reason why other people are the reason why some people cannot think for themselves.

However, when you think about this practice, it is also the same thing that governments, revolutions, and religious orders do. Some believe that they are leaders, and some make justification to themselves that they have the right to be tyrants. For that reason, you can establish that the people who engage with others and assume that they have control are the ones who have plenty of self-confidence.

Self-Esteem and Projection

People want to become someone that they aspire to become, and in the process starts the grand illusion of the reality that they are in. The very sense of self that people have enables them to play roles, but it is important to think that it is not often to their disadvantage. Some make it a point to play roles in order to achieve what they want in their lives.

Show mentalist Derren Brown wrote in his book, Tricks of the Mind, that what people mean to become is not really the people that they are. In saying this, he points out that what people communicate to others are the impressions that really matter. People do not really give importance to who people really are – rather, they give meaning to the messages that they receive through body languages, appearances, and conversations.

For this reason, many people make it a point to project themselves according to how they want other people to see them. A peace-loving man may make himself look like a thug so that people would not want to pick fights with him. A simple woman may want to wear makeup and high heels in the office to make her officemates think that she is pretty and sophisticated. As much as the idea that people are willing to accept people the way they really are is laudable, social standards of beauty, power, and intellect still shroud what others think of the people that they meet.

In the world of covert tactics of manipulation, deception, and mind control, self-esteem is also the foundation of mental superiority. It allows people to be able to devise tactics to issue control over others, and it also is the reason why they can build relationships with others using the self-image that they project. Some people who are not able to finish college can seem to have a Master's Degree. Some who do not have the money to buy a mobile phone can make people think that they have luxury cars. This is because these are the images of themselves that these people want other people to see, and they can make that happen with simple language implications. When you think about it, it is possible that other people do not really see you as you see yourself, but the person that you want to become.

The Self and Power

At this point, you would begin to understand that influence, manipulation, and deceit are forms of role playing – one plays as the manipulator, and the other, the manipulated. The question is this: who gets to decide what role goes to whom?

Here comes the idea of power play in the politics of control. A tactical influencer or manipulator is the one who can portray the image of authority, while the influenced or manipulated is often the one who wants to believe in another possible scenario. In this kind of scenario comes all the tactics of deceit, manipulation, and suggestion that would be discussed in this book.

It is also important to take note that a person's desires play a very important role in how manipulation tactics work out. While you may think that manipulators only think about everything that concerns them, what targets desire to hear or learn is crucial in making manipulative tactics work very well against them. When tactics are played to make it seem that what targets are hearing works to their advantage, they are very likely to subject themselves to manipulation to get what they want. When you think about it, some people do walk into the trap of being influenced to pursue their goals.

Now, why is it important that you know who you are in this kind of power play? Knowing when you are being manipulated or deceived allows you to choose whether you should participate in this role playing or not, and believe it or not, you have the power to make that decision. With enough self-esteem, you can tell yourself that you are not a puppet to obey commands or act without will. You can tell yourself that you can make your own decisions out of influences that you choose for yourself.

Chapter 4 - Understanding Manipulation

In almost every social aspect of humanity, a certain degree of manipulation is always present. Manipulation can be viewed as a motivating action that is aimed at influencing the decision-making process. This phenomenon is usually done indirectly. It can be so subtle that the person being manipulated can be totally unaware of its existence. It can also be made so deliberately that a person targeted to be manipulated would think that he has no choice but to make a decision he would not want to, but knows that he is not under duress and can make another decision.

Deliberately causing interference in the way other people think or behave is generally and is ethically questionable. The use of trickery methods like distractions, misdirection or temptations makes manipulation an undesirable means to obtain something. However, manipulation can take several different forms that the process of identifying it is a bit difficult.

The power of manipulation is undeniable. It is not persuasion, coercion or mere deception. It is an elusive and sophisticated method of influencing the behavior and mindset of another. Today, manipulation is just everywhere. It can be found in the education system, media, arts, politics, and even within intimate relationships. In addition, anyone can fall victim of such indirect means of control.

Despite the pervasiveness of the phenomenon of manipulation, the research and academic milieu paid too little attention to it. Only a few works exploring the nature of manipulation is available and known; hence, the entirety of the said phenomenon is still far from being crystal clear. This is the reason why there is still no universal definition used to describe manipulation until present.

There are, however, some authors offering definitions that can somehow help people grasp what manipulation is. For instance, Joel Rudinow described manipulation as follows;

"*A* attempts to manipulate *B* if *A* attempts the complex motivation of *B*'s behavior by means of deception or by playing on a supposed weakness of *B*" (Rudinow, 1978:88)

Robert Goodin provides another definition that tries to bring light to the manipulation phenomenon. He said that a person is manipulating another if he or she is deceptively influencing another, making the latter act opposite his putative will (Goodin, 1980).

The aforementioned definitions and others not mentioned are all concentrating on the unique characteristics of manipulation to stress its difference from other motivating actions. Apparently, most authors agree that manipulation is different from persuasion and even deception. Such characteristic can help narrow down the elusiveness of manipulation. Hence, the following entry is devoted to present more of what describes the said phenomenon to understand better what it is not.

What Manipulation Is

The word itself brings about the notion that manipulation is a motivating action. From a common perspective, manipulation is a process by which a person attempts to maneuver another person to a specific goal or behavior. As mentioned earlier, manipulation is usually done indirectly; hence, it can be expected that this phenomenon occurs in situations where parties hold contrasting views or perspectives.

Schools of thoughts, however, vary when it comes to interpreting what lies beneath the different views or perspectives of the parties involved in a social context where manipulation is taking place. Some claim that manipulation always works against the ones being manipulated. Such understanding places emphasis on the clashing interests behind the differing perspectives of the parties involved.

Nevertheless, there are authors claiming that the contradiction of the parties does not necessarily reflect opposing interests. For some, manipulation takes place because of the parties' contradicting wills. Such perspective, however, readily assumed that the manipulator has a clear knowledge of the other's will, which can be difficult to ascertain in a real life setting.

Another author stated that manipulation is a motivating action employed indirectly to avoid facing resistance if a rather direct approach will be utilized (Handelman, 2009).

Manipulation is not a manipulation if the target person is aware of it. Indeed, manipulation is always kept hidden from the knowledge of the target while it is taking place. This is another characteristic unique to manipulation. The manipulator's goal is to influence the other person's behavior and decision-making while the person is totally convinced that he or she is the one in control. For example, you may think that you are not influenced by anyone to read this book. However, you were compelled by a force to make reading this book a very rational choice. You are free to do what you want, but instead, you chose to sit there and read this passage.

Indeed, the person being manipulated must cling to the notion that he or she is acting based on his or her own resolve. Nevertheless, in reality the person being manipulated is geared to a decision or behavior that under normal circumstances, he or she would opt not to take. Such illusion of free choice is another property of manipulation (Handelman, 2009).

A skilled manipulator can bend the target person's mind and make him or her do even those things that are contrary to his or her perspective. Most of the time, the manipulator creates or stimulates a strong desire in the target's mind and embeds an impression that he or she is choosing right with the manipulator's indirect guidance.

Motivating actions like manipulation cannot be easily found in their purest forms. Even the act of deception contains some elements of truth in it. Hence, people even in the professional milieu find it difficult to clearly identify what makes manipulation different from other motivating actions like coercion and persuasion. The demarcation lines between and among the said motivating actions are still blurred.

For instance, where coercion ends and where manipulation starts is a problem commonly faced when trying to explore motivating actions. There exist no specific boundaries for each phenomenon. Klaidman and Beauchamp (1987) though, offered one helpful assessment. To make matters understandable, they placed motivation, coercion and persuasion in a continuum measured by the degree of controlling involved in the process. They placed manipulation in between the two extremes of lack of control - that is persuasion and the complete control of coercion (Klaidman & Beauchamp, 1987). Hence, manipulation is not persuasion or coercion, but something that lies in between the two.

Although commonly used as synonymous in the everyday expression, manipulation also differs from deception just like how it differs from coercion and persuasion. This can be measured using the level of "misleading" another person in the process. On one hand, coercion requires complete and intended misleading elements to function. On the other hand, manipulation is neither completely deceptive nor honest and it may contain different levels of misleading elements. Hence, it is once again situated in the gray area (Handelman, 1990).

Chapter 5 - Techniques on Manipulating Other People

Manipulation, once mastered, can really be a powerful tool for a person to achieve that which he or she desires. It is a motivating action that influences the critical capacity of a person. Such mechanism is the one responsible for making a person's behavior and decisions parallel to his or her preferences. This can be done by clouding or blurring the critical capacity of the person being manipulated (Handelman, 2009).

Appeal To Emotions

A particular technique utilized to accomplish manipulation successfully is the use of the description of Erich Fromm for manipulative technique - that is, by appealing to emotions and not to reason. This technique is commonly used in advertisements. By targeting the person emotionally, he or she will submit even intellectually.

A person's affectivity can really be a weak spot that most manipulators target. Emotions are just so powerful that they can bend reasons, standards or preferences.

Appeal to Authority

Another way to bypass a person's critical capacity is to use professional knowledge and expertise. This is a technique exploited by the modern market. It is very common nowadays for people to buy gadgets and devices that they do not truly understand. When a person steps in a shop, he or she may have some specific preferences in mind regarding what to buy. Nevertheless, it is a huge possibility that he or she will leave the shop with something different from what he or she originally wants.

Such scenario happens with the aid of a salesman's "expertise" and "knowledge." With his professionally sounding guidance on what to expect on products and some technical information that most people cannot really relate to, the salesman can easily manipulate the decision of buyers. The appeal brought by the expertise and technical knowledge of the salesman hides from buyers the fact that he is just emphasizing the good things about their product.

Indeed, the professional knowledge is an effective means to maneuver people into a certain direction. The same is true with some mathematical expertise or psychological knowledge.

Framing

Another technique that could cloud or paralyze a person's critical capacity in decision-making is by introducing a different solution to the same problem or by framing the issue in a different way. For instance, a choice problem can be viewed as a choice between losses or gains. If it is the choice between losses, the person is likely to choose the more risky option. However, if the same problem is presented as a choice between gains, the person will opt to stick with the less risky selection (Maoz, 1990).

Another way of framing is to make a target feel responsible for an action, as if they are privileged to make it. For example, a slogan that says "people should exercise the right" to vote makes less impact than a slogan that says "you should exercise your right to vote." By making a particular option look like an ownership, it becomes more valuable to the person who is asked to make it.

More Tips In Manipulating Others

"I need YOUR help..." this is perhaps the simplest yet most effective line to successfully get into the mind of someone. Indeed, making the person feel that he or she is needed makes him or her involved in the situation. Hence, the manipulator can make a person do something he or she would not normally do particularly for a stranger.

Another strategy is called social exchange. It is an unwritten rule that if person A does something for person B, no matter how small the favor is, person B is in turn compelled to return the favor in one way or another. Hence, to make a person pressured to comply with a certain request or favor, one must invest in giving something to that person first. The rather dark version of this exchanging of favors can take the form of blackmail. Hence, to no surprise, some people can easily abuse this technique.

Another commonly used technique of simple manipulation is the fear and then relief method. This is what lies behind the good-cop-bad-cop strategy. In this particular strategy, one is manipulating another using his or her emotions. Studies reveal that people who were exposed to stimulus arousing fear followed by a sudden stimulation of relief will experience some moment of being less likely to carry out rational decisions. This technique is also commonly utilized by insurance agents or even by mechanics.

Taking advantage of the mind shortcuts allows one to manipulate another. Human mind is wired to simplify things to avoid information overload. Hence, it is very common for people to resort to such simplified version of the world in dealing with their everyday life.

Consider how a person's behavior changes depending on the status of another person he or she is talking to. Such behavioral change can be induced by exploiting the person's use of his or her mental shortcuts. In making first impressions, mental shortcuts work most of the time. People are not all willing to spend time to get to truly know another person, instead they rely on their ready made expectations depending on how the person presents him or herself. Hence, by altering the way one dresses up and talks, he or she can steer people into behaving in a manner one desires them to do so.

Some studies reveal that in courts, suspects who present themselves neatly and nicely receive punishments that are less severe. This is because the judge resorts to mental shortcuts just like any other people do to carry out decisions. The judge does not have the luxury of time to thoroughly know the suspect; hence, he or she resorts to mental shortcuts as well, deciding from what he or she sees right in front of his or her eyes on the judgment day.

Types of Manipulation

Despite the availability of some data regarding manipulation, it still remains to be an elusive phenomenon. Such characteristic of ambiguity makes it possible for manipulation to take different shapes and forms. Indeed, there are just several guises that prevent the act of manipulation from being revealed and skilled manipulators can be as creative and subtle as possible.

Handelman (2009) describes four classifications of manipulation. The target person characterizes the first two in relation to the perceived freedom of choice and the last two are based on considerations that can be highly subjective or biased. By combining these four classifications, Handelman came up with four types of manipulation.

In relation to the perceived liberty in choosing, manipulation can be classified into limiting and expanding manipulation. Handelman states that limiting manipulation happens when the manipulator is narrowing down the choices leading the target person down to a single option. Directly opposing such strategy is the expanding manipulation, which is aimed at widening the target person's horizon instead of narrowing it down. This way, the manipulator can lead the target person away from something that he or she is trying to avoid or eliminate.

The intellectual and emotional classification of manipulation both involves the criterion of motivating effect. The intellectual manipulation is aimed at making a person use objective reasoning or rationalization to decide or act on something. The emotional manipulation, on the other hand, is making the person act automatically or impulsively by limiting the target person's capability to analyze and logically explain his or her actions (Handelman, 2009).

Chapter 6 - Understanding Deception

Just like manipulation, deception can take different forms of activities and concealments that aim to mislead the target person. The use of deception is not a new thing for the political and military milieu. It has been utilized for several decades already that it is now considered a traditional component of military and political conflict.

The objective behind every deception varies as much as its method of employment differs. It can be done in many different levels. Deception, just like manipulation, is a phenomenon that needs more attention from the academic and research milieu.

General Classifications

From what is known, there are some types of deception that can be utilized to control the will and mindset of another person. The first type is known as *strategic deception*. This is a deception done to cover up the basic intentions, capabilities, objectives and strategy of the deceiver. The second type is called *tactical deception*. In this kind of deception, the deceiver and the target person are actively participating in a certain competition. Misleading the target person away from the real interest or value of force involved is the goal of this kind of deception. The last commonly known type of deception is *operational deception*. This kind of deception confuses people to be able to covertly conduct a certain action or operation (Caddell, 2004).

In everyday experience, misleading another person and hiding the truth can be considered a common experience to most people. For the majority, their way of deception is in the form of lying. Such deception can also be employed in different manners. Although lying can be considered the most overused misleading technique, some people are still not good at it. This book is not trying to support the act of lying but for the sake of information, this book will discuss some ways on how to make lying more effective.

How Deception Becomes Effective

Deception in the form of lying is highly effective once it is done only when it is really needed. Using lies to mislead people over and over can increase the chances of being caught guilty of deception. Hence, only when there is a significant reason should a person resort to lying. In addition to this, it is rather easier to make people believe in something unreal when the person delivering the lies has never had a reputation of being a liar.

However, a liar can get away with his deceit when the truth that he is presenting is plausible. At a certain extent, a liar can even convert a lie into a false memory, making a re-imagination of events even easier. All that he needs to fabricate is a portion of the truth that everyone can agree with, and then turn the rest into a very compelling form of misinformation.

Planning ahead is also highly important. Constructing the lie prior to the announcement of it will help the person be consistent with the details and be aware of the possible loopholes of the fabricated information. Part of this plan must be the identification of the target person. To make the lie seamless, a person must know beforehand the perspectives of the person to be deceived. Learning things about the target person can help the deceiver avoid bringing matters up that could trigger suspicion.

How Difficult Is It To Lie?

Lying, generally, is not an easy task. Telling a lie requires more effort and stirs more emotions that when telling the truth. Aside from the consistency of the facts to be presented, a person must also be consistent with his or her expressions and gestures. A mixture of emotions including fear and remorse can affect the person's way of speaking and his or her non-verbal cues when lying.

For this reason, a liar tends to be self-conscious about the act itself, especially when he does not believe that he can pull a complete fabrication off. It is definitely not an easy task to create instant pictures in your head to make a compelling scene – your mind will need some time to create a reaction that you need when you are asked a question to prove that you are telling the truth. When you are trying to make another person focus on your version of the details, you also unconsciously try to make the other person notice other facts, rather than his doubt. Because of this, a liar tends to talk slower and increase the pitch of his voice at certain parts of his tale. He also makes unconscious movements whenever he tries to access a part of his mind where he is fabricating memories.

Hence, it is important for the person to practice delivering the fabricated information in front of the mirror to achieve the most convincing and naturally looking and sounding statement of lies.

Even in the art of lying, a well-developed self-esteem comes in handy. Indeed, the person's confidence can help in effectively covering up the misleading and deceiving intent intertwined with the fabricated information.

Exploring Deceptive Tactics

At this point, you are aware that deception is, generally, the act of not telling the truth. In nature, deception is a way for animals to protect themselves from danger and they do that in making their enemies perceive them as something else. In human beings, the motives for deception are particularly in the interest of both self-actualization and self-preservation – people are known to deceive because they need to protect what is important to them. However, there are many circumstances wherein human deception can be damaging because of the pursuit of personal interest.

For this reason, it is important to know what type of deception you are encountering in the most normal situations. Here are the deceptive tactics that you can expect to experience.

1. Lying

Lying is the deliberate fabrication of truth. Its foundation is the misinformation that the target receives which may be very different or the opposite of what is true. The story that the deceiver tells is being offered up as the truth.

2. Concealment

This is the act of omitting information that is relevant to the context of the truth. This includes exuding behavior that may prevent the target from knowing a particular piece of complete information.

3. Understatement

This is the act of downplaying relevant aspects of the truth to prevent the target from knowing a particular impact of an action or prevent suspicion of a negative outcome.

4. Exaggeration

This is the act of overstating particular parts of the truth to make some parts more important the other factors of the reality.

5. Equivocation

This is the act wherein the deceiver makes ambiguous, or even contradictory statements to make a false impression to his target.

By understanding when these tactics are taking place in a particular conversation, you will have a general idea that the information that is being presented to you is a fabrication or an altered version of the truth. When that happens, you know how to act accordingly, and even dig deeper to find out what the truth really is.

Chapter 7 - Understanding Mind Control

Among the acts that are aiming to influence another, mind control perhaps is the most controversial and the most frowned at method. Even some experts would consider mind control to be the most horrible crime for it is a crime committed against a person's mind. Influencing the actions, opinions and beliefs of people has caught the attention of both the state and the church long ago. However, it was only during the latter part of 1940s that the control of human mind in the complete form was managed (Bowart, 1978).

Mind control, however, is also the term used by several meditation groups to refer to contemplation, self-hypnosis and meditation. Such mind control processes are the ones seen to be beneficial as practitioners wanted to alter their own minds for the better. Nevertheless, the previously mentioned kind of mind control used by powerful forces in the society is geared towards controlling other people's mind with or without their consent and knowledge.

Brainwashing is a form of mind control that first came into the public's knowledge during the 1950s (Bowart, 1978). It was then a term used to describe the treatments received by American soldiers during the Korean War in the prison camp of the Chinese.

For what is known today, brainwashing can take the form of hypnosis. This technique brings on suggestibility on a higher level. It is the process of altering the consciousness state of the person. This process requires the ability to utilize verbal directions to lead a person into his or her state of consciousness where he or she turns highly receptive to directions or suggestions. Once the hypnotist was able to enter such phase, he or she can now make suggestions to make the target person break a bad habit or to make him or her do something he or she would not do automatically under normal circumstances.

Although it appears that the hypnotist is the sole person in control during the process, hypnosis is actually a two-way street. Indeed, the target person must allow the hypnotist to lead him or her to an altered state of consciousness. The reason behind this is the fact that if the target person is highly anxious about being hypnotized, the process might not work accordingly. Consequently, it is the hypnotist job to remove all the fears and doubts in the mind of the target person.

Digging Deeper on Hypnosis

Hypnosis is very popular. However, there are several myths about the said mind control technique that people still cling into. One of which is the belief that once hypnotized, the person will act against his or her will. Hypnosis is a technique with certain limitations. It is using the power of suggestion over a person in a highly receptive consciousness state. A person cannot be forced to act against his or her deeply embedded beliefs or values even in such an altered consciousness state.

Some people believe that hypnosis will not work on them because they are intelligent. This is another misconception. In actuality, people with great minds are better candidates for a successful hypnosis. Contrary to what others expect, it is not the weak minds that can easily be altered into a more receptive state but those with great minds.

Another myth about hypnosis is that a person being hypnotized is unconscious during the process. The altered consciousness state mentioned in many definitions appropriated for the term hypnosis talks about a state

33

similar to daydreaming. Hence, the person being hypnotized is far from being unconscious. He or she is actually aware of what is happening.

Some people also say that hypnosis can be very dangerous for a person can get stuck in it. In reality, a person being hypnotized can opt to come out of the process anytime he or she wants (Shuttleworth, 2004).

These are just some of the common misconceptions people still consider until the present. The underlying steps or mechanisms working underneath hypnosis cannot really be illustrated clearly and objectively. Hence, it is not surprising to have myths revolving around regarding the nature of the said mind control technique.

How Hypnosis Works

A successful hypnosis can be relatively easy if the target person is clear of any worries or uncertainties. For the hypnotist, there are certain factors that can influence the effectiveness of his or her employment of hypnosis. One significant factor is the level of self-esteem the hypnotist carries. Indeed, the best way for the hypnotist to readily eliminate the anxiety of the target person is by displaying an outstanding level of confidence in his or her abilities.

A hypnotist's self-esteem allows him to establish rapport with his target. Without rapport, a target would be very unlikely to cooperate with the hypnotist and close his mind to any suggestion. Most of the time, a hypnotist would opt to pace with his target and establish increasing awareness of his environment, making the target think that all suggestions made in each statement is naturally-occurring. Once rapport is established and the target believes every statement to be true, the hypnotist would then make suggestions to lead the target into making actions that would also seem to be natural. You will learn more about this trick in the next chapter.

Confidence alone, however, may not work accordingly. It is necessary for the hypnotist to couple it with preparation, practice and expert knowledge about the process of hypnosis. Sounding and looking like a professional hypnotist is also a significant factor to consider. A calming and soothing voice also influences the hypnosis process and this can be achieved through practice. It is also important to keep the tone of the voice monotonous all throughout. It is also very important for the hypnotist to recognize that all his actions would contribute to the result of the hypnotism. If he makes a sudden movement that does not fit in the reality that he is establishing in his target's mind, he may break the rapport that he has established earlier.

Several other mind control techniques are utilized by research organizations or government agencies. Some may even include the use of certain drugs and highly questionable means to completely control a person's mind. Consequently, ethical concerns about mind control techniques are endless. This is the reason why the big forces in the society are keeping their experiments regarding mind control their top secret.

Chapter 8 – The Power of Suggestion

Here is a tactic that is made to sway people to reveal more about themselves or make them become more willing to participate in mind manipulation or even hypnosis. This tactic is called suggestion, and is widely used by hypnotists and mentalists on their audience. However, what does it really mean to be suggestible?

What Suggestibility Is

There are times when you feel that a person that you are talking to is very compelling to the point that you believe everything that he says. You would even believe it if he says that there is such a thing as a unicorn and that he has evidence to prove it. There are also times when you feel that when a boss or a professor tells you to sing or dance, you just feel like automatically obeying without any objections. When these things happen, it means that you are suggestible.

When you are more open to suggestions to the point that you find yourself believing everything that another person says, your mind goes into the process wherein you feel that there are many things that are actually possible in this life, and that it is rather easy to convince yourself that what you are hearing or experiencing is real. You also make it a point to convince yourself that singing or dancing is much easier than people actually think. There is also a point wherein simple compliance is much easier to do than resisting a statement or an order.

However, it is easy to create memories, even when they are not true. This normally happens when someone becomes a recipient of false information – when false information incorporates its way into what the mind would perceive to be normal, then you create a memory of something that did not happen. Yes, the mind works in mysterious ways.

Belief as a Bendable Truth

There are many times wherein you might have convinced yourself that there is a ghost in a scary or creepy place that you have visited once, and you may even attest that you have seen it. However, if that "haunted" place was decorated differently and it looked a little cheery, would you think that there is a ghost there?

The human mind willfully accepts suggestions because they make action a lot simpler – instead of having to will decisions each time you face a particular scenario, it simply follows the suggestion that your environment tells it. When you encounter particularly creepy places, your mind automatically thinks that there is most likely a ghost there. When you go to a coffee shop, it automatically tells you that you want to order a latte, like always. Your mind simply adapts to the situations that you have already experienced, and then tells you what you would naturally do. Your memory of how you are able to do things makes it easier for you to decide what actions you should make. You can decide to do something else, but it is easier for you to simply do things that are already out of habit.

However, suggestions can become tools for manipulation. This is because the mind is also very capable of producing false memories based on the information that is presented to it by a manipulator. Within this information, a hidden instruction may be present, and it leads a target into making decisions that are actually subtly instructed for him to make.

How do false memories happen? All people are susceptible to these memories when they are told very plausible stories and then adapts to them. It is very possible for a person to become unsure of what is really happening because there is another person in the room that is feeding him plausible scenarios which makes him doubt what he is really experiencing. Because the other person is believable, even trustworthy, he bites the bait of manipulation and become convinced that it is his own decision.

Here is one of the most popular tricks in mentalism, a branch of trickery that makes people believe in the occult or the sheer powers of the mind. Hold a string that is holding a pendant above the palm of your hand, and using only your mind, will that string to move. Make it move clockwise and then counter clockwise. Again, using only your mind, make the pendant stop moving. If you are made to believe that the string will move, your fingers would begin making unnoticeable unconscious movement to make the string "follow" your mind's movement. However, without this belief, of course the string would not budge from its original position at all. With the power of suggestion that makes you believe that it is indeed possible for an inanimate object to move using only your mind, your entire body would make it a point that that belief would come into fruition.

The Power of Presupposition

Presupposition is a technique that makes use of suggestion which makes the target think that he has experienced a situation which may not have existed. It is called as such because the manipulator "supposes" the plausible scenario to the target, even though it is also very possible that he has experienced otherwise. The mind adapts to the suggestion within the presupposition and then makes the person do a predictable action.

For example, a witness' testimony may become very unreliable when his interviewers ask very leading questions. He may think that he has seen a very violent car crash when in reality, another car has only made a little bump against the sidewalk when he is asked "how hard did the car slam into the post?" There may not even be a post on the sidewalk at all! However, he would think that the car did slam into a post and make a clear description out of it because he is led by the interviewer into making this particular testimony.

You may also encounter presuppositions in TV commercials. Kellogg's Cornflakes once had a copy that says "Have you forgotten how good they taste?" which effectively makes your mind think that you have enjoyed this brand of cereals even though you have not bought it yet. The hidden instruction here is very obvious – that is you should buy this brand to "remind" yourself that you this made your breakfast enjoyable.

Pacing and Leading

Suggestions become very effective when they correspond to other factors that a person targeted for manipulation is experiencing. You do that by feeding a target various information that he agrees to – in this case, you are reading this book, feeling very comfortable in that chair that you chose to sit on.

Leading comes after pacing, which is that command that suggests what you would desire to do after you become aware of your environment, making it look like that it is a very natural course of action. For example, while you are reading this paragraph, you would feel that there is an ant crawling on the back of your neck, and the longer it crawls, you feel a strong urge to touch your nape.

What happens if you are given an outright command instead of pacing first? An outright command such as "Touch your nape." is a command that makes you think whether you should act on it or not. It makes you think twice about doing so because you have no reason to do so. However, getting the feedback that you want to do something about a supposedly uncomfortable feeling makes you want to do it. It is even more effective because it is connected to things that you already are doing.

Repetitive Language

It is possible for you to believe something that is false when you hear a suggestion over and over again. By being exposed to repetitive suggestions, your mind eventually creates a pattern of thinking that adapts to these suggestions.

You may notice how some of the catchiest commercials that you watch on televisions are the ones that are repeating on very specific intervals, until you memorize the message that they are telling you. At this point, you begin to repeat the message to yourself and then unconsciously decide to buy the product the next time you see it while you are shopping.

The Workaround

False memories can be your enemy, especially when you make the decision to stick to your version of the truth. The best thing that you can do to avoid giving in to false memories is to deduce whether you are being led into making decisions that would not be rational when you stick to what you know you have experienced. It is a tough job to retain your experiences, but it is possible to make sure that you remember events and experiences well. Simply organizing your thoughts about your experiences makes it a lot easier for you to remember and make independent decisions.

The same goes to repetitive messages – you have to keep in mind that no matter how "sticky" a suggestion is, it does not meant that you have to act on it, especially if it is a suggestion that is meant to make you do an action that you would normally not do under normal circumstances. By clinging to your original beliefs, you would be able to ward off these suggestions.

Chapter 9 – How Information Works Against You

This era makes it a lot easier for people to get information about other people, and while a good amount of information makes lives better, too much available information can cause harm to others. By letting other people know too much about you, you make yourself become prone to manipulation and deceit.

Take a look on how advertising and targeted media work – in order to make a particular product more appealing and sellable, companies need to know what their target market behaves. The more information they get, the more effective their advertisement and their products become.

Some people use the information that they get from other people to reveal their vulnerabilities and make them become more effective targets for manipulation and deceit. It also makes them more predictable, which enable manipulators to be more strategic about their tactics to lead their target into a specific course of action.

Unconscious communication is part of the commodity that every manipulator and deceiver out there craves, because it makes them know how to respond to unconscious responses of the people that they are targeting. However, learning how to read unconscious communication also allows you to learn how to protect yourself from being manipulated into doing things that you do not want or to be influenced into believing information that are not factual, but simply targeted to make use of your biases.

How People Unknowingly Reveal Information

You may have heard of criminals who steal information from their targets using the internet and looking at your social media accounts. However, there are many ways wherein people can covertly get information from you without you having to actually go online. Here are some of the tactics that they can use to extract information against your will.

1. Cold reading

The way you appear and act in public tells a lot of things about you. Your physical appearance, as well as your patterns of speech and outward behavior reveals a lot about your choices and your biases, even the location where you are from and your preferences on food!

Cold reading is the secret that lies in the heart of every psychic trick that you would encounter, and when done successfully, this tactic can make you think that your mind can be read by the person who has decided to make you a target. When a person can make you believe that he has complete knowledge of the information that you have in your mind, you are very likely to be manipulated by suggestions during that encounter.

Cold reading is also very effective on learning how receptive a person is on what you are saying and even reveal a general notion of what he has in mind. A person who is tapping his foot is likely to unconsciously reveal that he wants to get away. A person who tends to look away is usually trying to access a memory, and depending on where he gazes tells whether it is a fabricated or an actual one. At the same time, how a person unconsciously communicates also tells how a person is likely to be suggestible or not.

2. Language cues

There are a lot of verbal nuances that tell about a person's preference, which is something that you would make use of if you are in the field of sales. For example, a person who likes to use the words look, show, appear, or seem is most likely to listen to a very visual sales pitch and buy the product in the process.

3. Pitch reading

A person who raises his pitch or speaks louder often wants to draw attention, and the one that speaks in a hushed voice is someone who wants to become distant or withdrawn from the issue. This is also a good theory to work on when you want to spot concealment or a fabrication of truth, or if you want to know whether you have made a correct guess over information that another person tries to hide from you.

4. Speed of statement

You can easily say whether a person is becoming careful over the information that is being revealed to you when he slows down – it becomes a very difficult process for the mind to juggle from one thought to another, and when a person slows down, there is a big chance that he is not telling the truth. If you spot that a person slows down in one part of the story and then becomes quicker in the others, you may want to know what is really going on in his mind. The information that you want to extract is most probably in that part of his statement.

By learning these tricks, you enable yourself to learn how you can get information to your advantage and also prevent yourself from unknowingly revealing information that you do not want other people to know.

Chapter 10 – Fallacies People Fall For

Many people unconsciously make them neglect objectivity and then come to unhealthy conclusions about their daily lives because of logical fallacies that they encounter. These logical fallacies often make people make use of "careless" logic to prove a point, and falling for them makes anyone become victims of unexamined beliefs about the world that they are in.

The sad thing is that many people fall for them because of how they are delivered, and keep in mind that when a very fallacious statement is uttered with conviction, it is very easy for them to seem credible for the mind. Do remember that once, people believed that the world sits upon the shell of an extremely large tortoise just because powerful religious orders tell so. It is only upon careful examination that such false notions are disproved, and for this reason, it is crucial that people examine everything that is presented to them as fact in order to not fall for deception or sheer ignorance and disregard for logic.

Here are the most common fallacies that people usually fall for everyday.

1. Appeal to Pity

Humans have always recognized that they are highly-emotional beings, but in order to live an examined life with morals, it is important to use emotions with logic as well. When people fall for an appeal to pity (such as 1 Like = 1 Donation in social media), people may think that they are providing a solution to a problem, when they are actually not – they are simply manipulated using their emotions to do something to address their moral needs, but without helping their intended recipient.

When you encounter any tactic that appeals to emotions and you feel that you have a strong sense of responsibility regarding the situation that you are presented, the best way to have a logical action is to examine whether the proposed action would actually help. If you do not think that the action a manipulator is proposing would be the right solution, then you are probably being targeted using this fallacy.

Example: By sharing or liking this post, you can help children in Africa.

2. Ad Hominem

This fallacy can be translated as an "attack to person" which means that a manipulator is merely using another person's flaw to make an opposing point seem to be irrelevant. However, the manipulator does not make a point to refute the opposition using reasons that are actually relevant to the point that he is trying to make. Simply put, it is illogical to think that another person becomes less credible just because he is flawed, or has been associated to anything that is flawed. Rebuttals that simply do not stick to the facts are definitely not helping to make a solid point.

Example: Person A cannot make a testimony against Person B because Person A has cheated in exams before.

3. Circular Arguments

Circular arguments are statements that are made to make a point become viable by making a series of argument that simply loop back to the first evidence the manipulator has put across the table. Circular arguments do not welcome any other evidences of truth, and as the name suggests, it makes the entire argument simply run in circles.

Example: The Bible is the word of God because God said so – it is written in the Bible.

4. Appeal to Common Folk

This fallacy can be considered as surrendering to the status quo or norms that may not even be logical to begin with. However, since traditions and norms have stood against the test of the time, people believe that they are right and should not be questioned at all. At the same time, this fallacy is also made by manipulators to making their targets think that they share the same opinion since they are bound by similar circumstances.

Example: People in Town A always marry during June, therefore, it is the best month to get married.

Person A is a rich man with large estates that supports increase in taxes. However, as a person who, like common people, puts his pants on one leg at a time, all people in his town should also support tax increase.

5. Appeal to Definition

This is one of the fallacies that manipulators favor because it limits an argument to what dictionaries can define, which, disregards more controversial or other definitions that other people may uphold. In this fallacy, a person may uphold the belief that lexical dictionaries are absolute, without giving regard to other definitions or norms that may be used by other people.

Example: The dictionary does not mention that two people of the same sex can get married. Therefore, gay marriage is wrong.

6. Appeal to Celebrity

This is a fallacy wherein a manipulator may make use of a celebrity to make other people join the bandwagon of buying a particular product or adhering to a particular belief without examining what truly works for them. The main idea is to argue that a particular thing is very desirable because a popular figure endorses it or uses it.

Example: Tom Cruise like this peanut butter. Because Tom Cruise is really great in MI 6 and is your favorite actor, this is probably the best peanut butter in the world.

7. Appeal to Normality

This is one of the most common fallacies that people commit in order to justify their actions. With this fallacy, people think that it is okay to be in a specific condition or commit a particular action because it is considered normal in the society that they are in. Also, this fallacy makes people arrive to the faulty conclusion that everything that is normal is good.

Example: I am almost obese. This is practically normal in this country.

8. Hasty Generalization

This fallacy makes people think that they have gathered enough evidence to justify a belief because they have seen an example of it, but in reality, that example is not enough to reach a conclusion that they desire.

Example: Your grandfather has lived up to a hundred years and he smokes. Therefore, cigarette smoking must not be that harmful to one's health.

9. Constitutional Rights Fallacy

There are times when people think that their rights do not have limits because the law is absolute. However, this is a fallacy, and a very common one. People who tend to commit this fallacy often think that laws, especially their rights, exist on a vacuum, and then make them invincible and not guilty of committing any offense.

Example: Trolling on the Internet is a constitutional right.

10. Strawman Fallacy

This fallacy is committed when you make an interpretation of another person's statement to mischaracterize it and make it easier to attack and prove wrong.

Example: Person A does not believe in religion. Therefore, he thinks that humans came from monkeys.

The Danger of Fallacies

Fallacies make it harder for people to make informed decisions and interpretations of every statement or occurrences that happen around them. By simply falling back to inconclusive and poor arguments to support claims or counter-claims, people often make mistakes of being influenced to make choices that they would not have chosen if they have a more accurate view of what they experience.

When you think about it, knowledge is largely based on how you experience the world around you and how you interpret it using the language that you know. However, mischaracterization of truth also appears in language, and this is the secret weapon of manipulators and deceivers. Without realizing whether the point that people around you is a fallacy or not, you may be preventing yourself to get accurate information. When that happens, you become manipulated and you may even defend your choices using the poor line of reasoning that you have heard.

Believe in Reason

At this point, you may realize that it is extremely difficult to combat manipulation, deception, and mind-control. It seems that the odds are against you, especially since most of the techniques that are used to practice these covert tactics are often downplayed as the norm. However, remember that you have the right to protect yourself from being influenced.

The first step to freeing your mind from the manipulation and lies is to be vigilant about the tactics that are mentioned in this book. At the same time, do not be afraid to question influence. Manipulators and deceivers may use a fallacy or two to misdirect you from your conviction, but make use of your self-esteem. Believe that you are worthy enough to be informed correctly – it is your right, and having the ability to defend your beliefs and question information is part of your free will.

Conclusion

Thank you again for purchasing this book!

I hope this book was able to help you to find the strategy that best fits you to in influencing other people's mind and behavior.

The next step is to apply the techniques discussed in this book to help others break a bad habit or to achieve your goals in life. You must, however, keep in mind that influencing human mind is an act that gives you certain responsibilities that you have to honor.

Finally, if you enjoyed this book, please take the time to share your thoughts and post a review on Amazon. We do our best to reach out to readers and provide the best value we can. Your positive review will help us achieve that. It'd be greatly appreciated!

Thank you and good luck!

www.ingramcontent.com/pod-product-compliance
Lightning Source LLC
Chambersburg PA
CBHW070829290526
45795CB00002B/886